Children's
Poems

This book was previously published in a larger format with a different cover.

Cover Design: Hannah Ahmed.

The publishers wish to thank all the poets for permission to reproduce their poems in this book.

The publishers have made every effort to trace copyright holders and would be grateful to hear from any not here acknowledged. This edition first published in 2003 by Usborne Publishing Limited, Usborne House, 83-85 Saffron Hill, London, EC1N 8RT, England. www.usborne.com This collection © Usborne Publishing Ltd. 2003, 1990. The individual copyrights belong to the authors. The illustrations © Usborne Publishing Ltd. 2003, 1990. The name Usborne and the devices ⊕ and ⊖ are Trade Marks of Usborne Publishing Limited. All rights reserved. No part of this publication may be stored in a retrieval system or transmitted in any form or by any means, electronic, mechanical, photocopy, recording or otherwise, without the prior permission of the publisher.

Printed in Spain

Children's Poems

Illustrated by Stephen Cartwright
Compiled by Heather Amery

Poems by
Dave Calder, Tony Charles, Elizabeth Chorley, Stanley Cook,
Pie Corbett, John Cotton, Peter Dixon, Gina Douthwaite,
Gavin Ewart, John Foster, Kenneth Grahame, David Harmer,
Trevor Harvey, Libby Houston, Michael Johnson, Kavin McCann,
Shelagh McGee,Robin Mellor, Trevor Millum, Brian Moses,
Judith Nicholls, Julie O'Callaghan, Irene Rawnsley,
Vernon Scannell, Matt Simpson,Anthony Smith,
Robert Louis Stevenson, Sue Stewart, Matthew Sweeney,
Marian Swinger, Charles Thomson, Roger Tulk.

With thanks to Lois Beeson

Up and away

Little Daisy Dittersdorf
  Decided she would fly:
"I'll make some wings and flap them
  And tootle round the sky!"

She fetched some bits of bamboo
  To make herself a frame
Which she covered up with silver foil
  Then painted on her name.

She strapped the wings upon her back
  And balanced on the fence.
She said "I'm going to go to Zanzibar!"
  We haven't seen her since.

Matt Simpson

Turning Points

Yesterday
Our teacher
Told us the story   "That's nothing!"
Of Lot's wife   Said Tracey Saunders.
Who looked back   "My mum was backing the car
And was turned   And when she looked round
Into a pillar of salt.   She'd turned into a ditch!"

John Foster

4

Enquire Within

"Is there anybody there?" asked the pupil,
Knocking on the staffroom door.
"You'll be lucky!" the cleaner answered,
"It's almost ten minutes past four!"

Trevor Harvey

My Sister's Knitting

My sister's sitting knitting
Each day she'll sit and knit,
Clicking garments into shape,
Wondering who they'll fit.
Long johns for Uncle Arthur,
Who tends to feel the cold,
(It's one of the discomforts
Of being rather old).
Short socks for Cousin Doris,
Who does a lot of walking;
A muffler for Gladys
Who does a lot of talking.
For Grandmama a bonnet,
(Two plain, three purl, slip one),
And this round thing's a cushion
For the cat to sit upon.
My sister's sitting knitting,
and I am all agog
To see my sister fitting
Woolly bloomers on the dog!

Shelagh McGee

5

Leonora

Leonora the Terrible
gritted her teeth
and, as she ran,
crushed three boys beneath
her pounding feet.
She crossed the yard
with seven league steps
and ignited the staffroom
with her fiery breath.
Her attention then turned
to the teachers who
were running about
not knowing what to do.
She opened her mouth
and with a dreadful roar
said, *I won't come to
your school, any more!*

Robin Mellor

Old Mother Hubbard

Old Mother Hubbard
Sat in the cupboard
Eating Jack's Christmas pie;
He opened the door
Gave a furious roar
And blacked Mother Hubbard's right eye.

Vernon Scannell

6

Sunday in the Yarm Fard

The mat keowed
The mow cooed
The bog darked
The kigeon pooed

The squicken chalked
The surds bang
The kwuk dacked
The burch rells chang

And then, after all the dacking and the chang-ing,
The chalking and the banging,
The darking and the pooing,
The keowing and the cooing...
There was a mewtiful beaumont
Of queace and pie-ate.

Trevor Millum

The Young Lady of Lynn

There was a young lady of Lynn,
Who was so uncommonly thin
That when she essayed
To drink lemonade,
She slipped through the straw and fell in.

Anon

7

Elephantastic

Six great grey elephants
were taking tea with me:
Mmmm, jungle sandwiches and savannah scones.
   Brr Brr Brr Brr
The quiet one went to take a trunk-call telephone.

Five great grey elephants
were taking tea with me.
A mammoth munching, scrunching session;
   Chomp Chomp Chomp
Then the loud one left for special trumpet lessons.

Four great grey elephants
were taking tea with me:
sticky stalks, fruit bursting at the seams.
   Squeaking speaking!
The small one heard a mouse. He ran away to scream...

Three great grey elephants
were taking tea me me.
Finished, bulging fat, sitting back, relaxed.
   Smash Splinter Crash
The big one's garden chair suddenly collapsed.

Two great grey elephants
were taking tea with me:
seven heaven-empty plates, seven heaven-empty cups.
   Splish Splash Splosh
Gigantic had a nosey-hose way of washing up.

8

One great grey elephant
is drying plates and cups and cutlery.
An extra-extraordinary sight for me to see?
   No No No No
No, because I'm a great grey elephant. Yes, me.
   Perhaps Maybe
Or was it just my tea-time elephantasy?

Michael Johnson

Little Bo Peep

Little Bo Peep has lost her sheep,
Her marbles, too – it could make you weep –
Dozy Boy Blue has gone to sleep;
Jack and Jill can't stay on their feet.

Spratt and his wife have nothing to eat.
Miss Muffet's scared of a harmless spider,
Contrary Mary? Who could abide her?
The Piper's son is a common thief
Who fully deserves to come to grief.

I bet Tommy Tucker's voice was a pain –
As bad as that kid's who howled in the lane.
So why pick on Simon? Simple? He
Doesn't seem as daft as the others to me!

Vernon Scannell

9

Big-head Dragon

O there once was a dragon
Who was given to braggin',
Who would bawl and would yell
        At
           the top of
              his
                 voice:

"I'm a rather swish dragon
With my spikey tail waggin';
Assume from the flames
              That
                my breath's
                      very
                         choice!

I munch lots of maidens
That I snatch on my raidin's;
I gobble them down
            With
              my
             bulldozer
                 jaws!

I'm a gorgeous green monster,
I'm a son-of-a-gun, sir,
With teeth yucky-yellow
            But
              as fierce
                as
                  sharp saws.

Should any daft knight, sir,
Step into my sight, sir,
I'll freeze his blood cold
            With my
              lasering red
                 eyes!

I'm a smasher, I'm terrific,
I'm as great as the Pacific,
Chomping off the heads
        Of those tin can guys!"

Matt Simpson

I Didn't Mean To

I didn't mean to spill the milk
Or break a dinner plate.
I didn't mean to kick the cat
Or come home very late.

I didn't mean to tear my dress
Or lose the front door key
I didn't mean to lie a bit.
You're always blaming me.

I didn't mean to frighten Gran
Or pull away her chair.
I didn't mean to burn the toast,
Get butter in my hair.

I didn't mean to make Mum cross
Or eat up all the cakes.
I didn't mean to make excuses
But everyone makes mistakes.

Elizabeth Chorley

The Flying Spring Onion

The flying spring onion
  flew through the air
    over to where
the tomatoes grew in rows
  and he said to those
    seed-filled creatures
My rooted days are done,
  so while you sit here
    sucking sun
I'll be away and gone,
  to Greenland
    where they eat no green
    and I won't be seen
in a salad bowl with you,
  stung by lemon,
    greased by oil,
and nothing at all to do
  except wait to be eaten.
With that he twirled
  his green propellors
and rose above the rows
  of red balls
who stared as he grew small
  and disappeared.

Matthew Sweeney

I Had a Little Brother

I had a little brother
His name was Tiny Tim,
I put him in a bath tub
To teach him how to swim.

He drank up all the water,
He ate up all the soap,
He died last night
With a bubble in his throat.

In came the doctor,
In came the nurse,
In came the lady
With the alligator purse.

"Dead," said the doctor,
"Dead," said the nurse,
"Dead," said the lady
With the alligator purse.

Out went the doctor,
Out went the nurse,
Out went the lady
With the alligator purse.

Anon

12

Problems with the Moon

When the moon fell into our garden
it took an awful lot of my
pushing and shoving
and swearing from Dad
to get it back up in the sky.

First we all leaned shoulders to it
and pushed when Dad called "Heave her";
it wouldn't move and Mum stepped back
suggesting we use a big lever.

So Dad got a plank from the garage
and I got one from the shed;
we tried them both, and the moonbeams rolled
right over Mum's best flower bed.

"Oh drat!" said Mum in anger,
"The blessed thing!" said Dad,
the moon slipped on to his greenhouse
and the things he said then were pretty bad.

Eventually our efforts succeeded
and, as Dad gave a mighty roar,
the moon shot up and outwards
and lodged in the sky once more.

Yes – when the moon fell into our garden
it took an awful lot of my
pushing and shoving
and swearing from Dad
to get it back up in the sky.

Robin Mellor

13

I Was Just...

I was just
Teaching our cat to swim
And suddenly
The bathroom was flooded.

I was just
Looking at Dad's razor
And suddenly
Our cat had a bald patch.

I was just
Seeing if our cat could fly
And suddenly
There's a hole in the shed roof.

I was just
Wondering if our cat had nine lives:
It didn't.

I was just wondering
What's the worst feeling in the world?
And now I really know.

Kevin McCann

Doing Topics

At School we do Topics.
I always do "Birds".
I quite like the drawings
but can't do the words.

Pie Corbett

Tall Story

He lives in the chimney
since he grew so tall
he couldn't fit
inside the house at all;

Dad takes a ladder
round to the back;
feeds my brother
at the chimney stack.

He likes an umbrella
when a wet wind blows
and woolly socks
to warm his toes

and we take it in turn
when the weather's fine
to sit on the roof
and talk to him.

But we don't like
the comments people make;
you'd think sometimes
it was our mistake

having a tall person
in the family;
my brother's
an ordinary you or me;

So we're going to move,
where living's cheaper;
Dad's got a job
as a lighthouse keeper.

Irene Rawnsley

15

ORChestra

What's that sound undelightful –
A noise fiendish and fightful –
Like the wailing of ghouls at the moon?
As the gruesome sound grows,
You wince, curl your toes...
It's the orc orchestra rehearsing its tunes!

The string section stands:
A bristling band
Of warriors of the night;
Their violins raised,
Their bug-eyes glazed
With musical delight.

A fearsome troll
Gives a fine drum roll
And a gremlin plays the tuba;
The orc octet
Play their clarinets
Like they were sticks of rhubarb.

There's a group of elves
Who hold themselves
With grandeur and with grace...
They play trombones
And finger-bones
At a fine foot-tapping pace.

There's a minotaur,
Who straddles the floor
And snorts through his great bull-nose;
And he grasps the bass
Like a battle mace
Smack-thwacking through his foes.

The woodwinds soar,
The flugelhorns roar
And the conductor swirls his stick,
While the dwarves play flutes
And lilting lutes
Allegro – or pretty quick!

Oh, now, don't be dismayed
At the way they play;
They really aren't going to bite you!
They may seem ferocious
And their music atrocious
But - they're doing their best to delight you!

Trevor Millum

The Young Lady of Riga

There was a young lady of Riga,
Who rode with a smile on a tiger;
They returned from the ride
With the lady inside,
And the smile on the face of the tiger

Anon

I Don't Want To Shrink

I don't want to get smaller,
I don't want to shrink,
if I wash too much I'll be
washed down the sink.
Mum keeps on saying
"Go and have a good wash."
But if I'm clean all the time
I'll look shiny and posh.
Have you seen what happens
to soap in the bath?
It gets smaller and smaller,
no... don't laugh,
it isn't funny to be washed away,
to get withered and wrinkled,
to disappear down the sink.
I don't want to get smaller,
dirt does me no harm,
I don't want to shrink. Anyway,
dirt keeps me warm.

Robin Mellor

Into the Mixer

Into the mixer he went,
  the nosy boy,
into the mess of wet cement,
  round and round
  with a glugging sound
and a boyish screamed complaint.

Out of the mixer he came,
  the concrete boy,
onto the road made of the sam
  quick-setting stuff.
  He looked rough
and he'd only himself to blame.

Matthew Sweeney

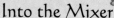

Call in the Vet

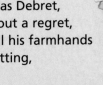

Sir Silas Debret
had to call in the vet
When the pigs in the sty
Turned blue.

"Dear Doctor," he sighed,
"I think someone's dyed
My especially imported
Pig stew!"

The vet took his soap,
A large stethoscope
And went in the sty
For a look.

Yes, the pigs were quite blue
And just what to do
Didn't appear
in his Book.

He thought and he thought
More than he ought,
Until he came up with
The answer.

"If I may be so bold,
These pigs are too cold!
What they need is some
Warm woolly pants, sir!"

Sir Silas Debret,
Without a regret,
Set all his farmhands
A-knitting,

Till after two Sundays
The pigs' thermal undies
Were finally ready
For fitting.

Even though it was snowing,
Soon the pigs were all glowing
And the snowflakes
Just melted away.

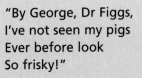

They all looked so pink
You couldn't help think
Of cherry trees
Blossoming in May.

"By George, Dr Figgs,
I've not seen my pigs
Ever before look
So frisky!"

Beamed Sir Silas Debret
Shaking hands with the vet
And pouring him out
Some malt whisky.

Matt Simpson

19

An Unspelling Bea

An unspelling bea, an unspelling bea
i buzz abart for ours u sea
Amungst blewbells and croakuss
And other flours, not making a fuss
As i serch for hunny and land on pedals
Making shore that nobody medals
With this sharp stinging
Humming-singing
Unspelling bea
Who seems to have lost his dictionree!

John Cotton

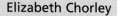

Pardon!

My mother stared,
My father glared,
I hung my head in shame.
But in the next long quiet bit,
I burped
and burped again.

Elizabeth Chorley

An Atrocious Pun

A major, with wonderful force,
Called out in Hyde Park for a horse.
All the flowers looked round,
But no horse could be found,
So he just rhododendron, of course.

Anon

Our Teacher

Our teacher taps his toes,
keeping the beat to some silent tune,
only he knows.

Our teacher drums his fingers,
on his desk, on the window,
on anything, when the room is quiet,
when we're meant to be writing,
in silence.

Our teacher cracks his knuckles,
clicks his fingers, grinds his teeth,
his knees are knocking the edge of his desk,
he breathes to a rhythmical beat.

When he turns his head in a certain way,
there's a bone that cracks in his neck.
When he sinks to the floor,
we often think, he'll stay on his knees
forever more, he's such a physical wreck!

Our teacher bangs his head against the wall
(or pretends to) when Wendy comes up
with another dumb remark.

Our teacher says we annoy him
with all our silly fuss.
Perhaps he's never really thought
how much he irritates us.

Brian Moses

21

Stop Me If You've Heard It Already

Once upon a time
in a kingdom far away
there lived an old old woman
in a gingerbread café.
She had three strapping sons
two ugly daughters who told lies
and a beautiful sad stepdaughter
who was a giant in disguise.
Now one day a knight passed by
running off to sea with a kipper
and dropped a golden frog
that laid a talking slipper
which the youngest son then sold
for a magic mashed potato
that ate his elder brothers
and began to grow and grow.
It put the young boy on its back
and flew off across the fields;
his sisters pedalled after it
on their spinning wheels.
They crossed a soggy river
they climbed a glass beanstalk
they caught that bad potato
with a knife and fork.
It turned into a princess,

and such was their surprise
the beautiful sad stepdaughter
grew forty-nine feet high
and the other sisters, curtseying,
(for they were awful snobs)
were squashed beneath her giant feet
into two shapeless blobs.
And when the old old woman
saw this on her TV
she sent a storm that drowned the
                                knight
that very night at sea.
The storm came roaring back again
and with a mighty clout
it knocked the old old woman
upside down and inside out.
It wrapped the giant in a cloud
and drowned it in despair
which made the son dissolve in tears
and vanish in thin air.
The poor potato-faced princess
was crushed by this disaster
and then there was nobody left at all
to live happily ever after.

Dave Calder

The Painting Lesson

"What's THAT dear?"
asked the new teacher.

"It's Mummy," I replied.

"But mums aren't green and orange!
You really haven't TRIED.
You don't just paint in SPLODGES
– You're old enough to know
You need to THINK before you work...
Now – have another go."

She helped me draw two arms and legs,
A face with sickly smile,
A rounded body, dark brown hair,
A hat – and, in a while,
She stood back (with her face bright pink):
"That's SO much better – don't you think?"

But she turned white
At ten to three
When an orange-green blob
Collected me.

"Hi, Mum!"

Trevor Harvey

23

Conversation with an Alien

Well, I was sitting in the garden,
the day was nearly done,
and I lounged about on the patio
in the rays of the setting sun,
when up above, and to the right,
I heard a wheezing sigh,
like that thte baby tends to make
when he is going to cry.

So I looked up and there I saw,
dropping down from the sky,
a sort of blue teapot without a lid
and I wondered that it could fly.
It landed right in front of me,
in the middle of the garden,
a door slid open and out he came,
a *Thingy*, if the expression you'll pardon.

With curiosity I looked at him
and from my seat I rose,
walked over, smiled, and nervously said,
"You're invading us, I suppose?"
He looked at me, looking at him,
I looked at him as he looked at me,
he was green (of course) and spiky too
with three legs and yellow knees.

"What is your name?" I said to him,
he answered not a word.
The Alien and I stood silently,

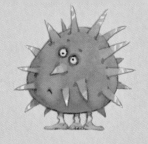

It was really quite absurd.
So slowly I repeated my words
and asked the question again,
"You're from outer space, I can see," I said,
"Please, will you tell me your name?"

And he said, "Bleebleoople,"
and I said, "Pardon?"
And he said, "Bleebleoople,"
and I said, "What?"
And he said, "Bleebleoople,"
and I said, "Oh."

"So, what have you come for?" I asked.
"Trippledizzies, slippleoodle," he said,
and I said, "Pardon?"
"Trippledizzies, slippleoodle," he said,
and I said, "What?"
"Trippledizzies, slippleoodle," he said,
and I said, "Oh."

"So where are you from?" I asked,
And he said, "Trimpleslicksness,"
and I said, "Pardon?"
And he said, "Trimpleslicksness,"
and I said, "What?"
And he said, "Trimpleslicksness,"
and I said, "Oh."

He turned back to his space ship,
"Where are you going?" I cried,
And he said, "Ziproodlooses,"
and I said, "Pardon?"
And he said, "Ziproodlooses,"
and I said, "What?"
And he said, *"You Humans never
listen!"*
and I said, "Oh...
...goodbye."

Robin Mellor

To the Moon

O Moon! when I look on your beautiful face
Careering along through the darkness of space,
The thought has quite frequently come to my mind
If ever I'll gaze on your lovely behind.

Anon

Big Boots

Suppose I wore
size ninety-nine boots,
I'd walk in mud
wherever I found it.

I'd make a trail of footprints
down the street
so that people
would say,
Let's hurry away;
a giant
or a monster
or a yeti
or a dinosaur
or a great big
hairy gorilla
came this way!

I'd keep my boots
in the garden shed,
and hang my big feet
out of bed.

Irene Rawnsley

The Strawberry Cried

The strawberry cried
"I'm in a jam!
I don't know why
But here I am."

The little tart
Said, "So I see.
I know because
the jam's in me."

And Tubby Tibbs,
The greedy lad,
Devouring both
Said, "Just too bad!"

Vernon Scannell

The Man of Bengal

There once was a man of Bengal
Who was asked to a fancy dress ball;
He murmured: "I'll risk it
and go as a biscuit..."
But a dog ate him up in the hall.

Anon

26

Please Sir!!

There's a fight – Sir!!
In the cloakrooms... Sir!!
And Arnie's strangled Paul.
Smithy's strangled Watson
'cos Watson took his ball.
Barney's ripped his shirt... Sir,
And Baker spat on Sue.
She was only tryin' to stop them
And she's got it on her shoe...
The helper lady went... Sir,
She said she couldn't stay.
Jane's crying in the toilets
And the gerbil's got away....

Garnett knocked the cage... Sir,
The door, it just flipped back,
And it ran behind the cupboard
And it's stuck inside a crack.
We poked it with a stick... Sir,
But the powder paint got spilt.
It's over all the carpet
And it's over Helen's kilt.
I think you ought to come... Sir,
Mildred Miles was sick
And all the boys are yellin'
And Martin threw a brick.
It nearly hit John Baily.
And he's goin' to tell his mum,
So shall I say you're comin'
and shall I fetch his mum?

Shall we get the cleaners?
And can I mop the paint?
The new boy's torn his jacket
And he thinks he's going to faint...
The other teachers said... Sir,
That I should come to you
'Cos you're the Duty Teacher
        So you'll know what to do
                              Sir.

Peter Dixon

27

Father's Race

Tony's dad goes jogging,
Gareth's dad lifts weights.
Leroy's dad's a stunt man,
Errol's dad jumps gates!

Trixie's dad plays football
for a fourth division team.
Rachel's dad's a sprinter,
fast and flash and lean.

But my dad's thin and weedy
he's bound to lose the race.
He'll stumble and trip or worse,
fall flat upon his face.

Simon Miller's dad
enters marathons.
I've seen him training hard,
running from Simon's mum!

I know my friends will laugh
and call me awful names.
Please don't enter the race, Dad,
it's me who gets the blame!

Brian Moses

The Old Lady of Rye

There was an old lady of Rye
Who was baked by mistake in a pie,
To the household's disgust
She emerged through the crust,
And exclaimed, with a yawn, "Where am I?"

Anon

The Sleuth

I longed to be a Private Eye
But there were hordes of those;
So I filled a gap in sleuthing work
And became – a Private Nose.

I sniffed out clues as best I could,
But didn't do too well;
It was because I'd overlooked
I lacked a sense of smell.

"You're just a Drip!" my clients cried.
"Why did we pick a Nose?"
I thus gave up on nostril work
And became – a Set of Toes.

I crept about to stalk my prey
Who didn't give "two hoots";
They knew EXACTLY where I was –
I'd put on squeaky boots.

From Private Nose to Private Toes,
My life has been a failure!
I wonder if they're short of Eyes
In Hong Kong – or Australia?

Trevor Harvey

29

Peasy!

You want me to do that ten figure sum,
      that's peasy!
Wind my legs over that bar,
slide down into a forward roll
with a double back flip to follow,
      that's peasy!
Build a working model of Big Ben
from Technical Lego,
Huh, peasy!
Clear that five foot hurdle in one leap,
cross country run up a mountain peak,
keep writing a story for one whole week,
      peasy!
Score thirty goals in record time,
in ten minutes write a thousand lines,
say "Supercalifragilisticexpialidocious" two hundred
times, backwards,
      Oh that's peasy!
BUT...
eat the skin off of custard.
Ugh! That's the toughest thing in the world!

Brian Moses

Did You Ever Go Fishing?

Did you ever go fishing on a bright, sunny day?
Sit on a fence and have the fence give way?
Slide off the fence and rip your pants,
And see the little fishes do the hootchy-kootchy dance?

Anon

30

The Great Computer

Professor Ditherspoon-Wombat,
Working all alone,
Built the greatest computer
The world had ever known.

He made micro-chips from potatoes
And his dolly mixture transistors
Were all linked up with chewing gum
And hair grips of his sister's;

Got a mega-byte from a dinosaur,
From a bi-plane unbolted a joystick,
Made floppy discs from a halibut
And a keyboard out of Blu Tack.

And when he had constructed it
Quite to his satisfaction
He decided he would type in
Some very knotty questions.

For example: how many beans make five?
How does your garden grow?
How much is that dog in the window?
Where do flies in winter go?

The answer to the first one
Came out as "93",
To the second: "Oh, the usual!"
To the third: "As much as me!"

But when it tried to work out
The answer to Question Four
Its fuses flew like fireworks
And it melted all over the floor.

31

Ambrose Visits His Aunt

When Ambrose went to visit his aunty
it was for the very first time;
he wanted to make a good impression,
wanted the afternoon to be fine.

But he tripped when he stood on the doorstep
and banged his head on the door,
so when his aunty opened it up
he was lying on the floor.

She took him into the kitchen
to have a cup of tea,
he sat on the cat (asleep on the chair)
and caught the table with his knee.

This jogged the cups and saucers
and spilt the milk on the cloth,
the teapot teetered on the edge
and, with a crash, it fell right off.

Ambrose bent to pick up the pieces
and slipped on the tea stained floor,
flattened the jugs on the dresser
and put his foot through the door.

At this point in the proceedings
his uncle came into the room
and looked at the chaos around him
with a face that looked like Doom.

Ambrose said that he would help them
to clear the mess he had made,
but they tied him to an armchair
and gave him some lemonade.

No further catastrophe happened,
for they wouldn't let Ambrose move,
and when he said "Thanks for having me,"
his aunt said something rude.

Ambrose waved goodbye to his aunty
and started on his way home;
he walked carefully down the narrow path
and fell over a garden gnome.

Robin Mellor

Not a Word

They walked the lane together,
The sky was dotted with stars.
They reached the rails together,
He lifted up the bars.
She neither smiled not thanked him,
Because she knew not how,
For he was only the farmer's boy
And she was the jersey cow!

Anon

The Boy Stood in the Supper-Room

The boy stood in the supper-room
Whence all but he had fled;
He'd eaten seven pots of jam
And he was gorged with bread.

"Oh, one more crust before I bust!"
He cried in accents wild;
He licked the plates, he sucked the spoons –
He was a vulgar child.

There came a burst of thunder-sound –
The boy – Oh! where was he?
Ask of the maid who mopped him up,
The bread crumbs and the tea!

Anon

The Centipede's Song

Forty thousand little legs
Walking down the stairs,
Forty thousand little feet,
Walking down in pairs.

Crunching on the gravel,
Marching in the shade,
Sounding like an army
Of soldiers on parade.

How happy are the centipedes
Who do not have a care,
Except to keep their thousands
Of boots in good repair.

Anon

34

Duck's Ditty

All along the backwater,
Through the rushes tall,
Ducks are a-dabbling,
Up tails all!

Ducks' tails, drakes' tails,
Yellow feet a-quiver,
Yellow bills all out of sight,
Busy in the river!

Slushy green undergrowth
Where the roach swim –
Here we keep our larder,
Cool and full and dim!

Every one for what he likes!
We like to be
Heads down, tails up,
Dabbling free!

High in the blue above
Swifts whirl and call –
We are down a-dabbling,
Up tails all!

Kenneth Grahame

I've Got a Dog As Thin As a Rail

I've got a dog as thin as a rail,
He's got fleas all over his tail;
Every time his tail goes flop,
The fleas on the bottom all hop to the top.

Anon

A Twentieth-Century Fox

The field is a pool of silver
a bright disc cut by the moon.

A grinning star
steps into the spotlight.

His woodland audience are tense
hold their breath, close their eyes.

They wish he would disappear
vanish like Dracula into his coffin.

But he begins to strut and dance
caper around on neat black feet.

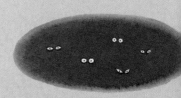

His ginger wig and savage mask
disguise his eyes in the moonlight.

He relaxes, enjoys his act
scaring the audience to death.

David Harmer

Algy Met a Bear

Algy met a bear,
A bear met Algy.
The bear was bulgy,
The bulge was Algy.

Anon

Please, Noah!

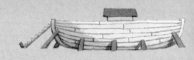

Tortoise

I'm slow, Noah,
slow.
Don't put me near the hare,
the horse's hoof,
the elephant.
I fear...
the python, Noah;
his curling tongue
is long enough
to pierce my home.
Let me share my room
with mole, light-footed wren
or snail; he cannot stamp
or run. Best of all,
just let me be
alone.

Mouse

Am I the smallest, Noah?
Is it a trap?
Please, I'd like
cheese to gnaw
and nuts to nibble.
I won't quibble
if I have to share
with gerbil, guinea pig
or even rabbit, hare...
but please, not *cat*!
Dear Noah,
whatever else,
not *that*!

Sloth

Sleep, Noah,
about my sleep.
I see it's going to be
quite hard for me
to sleep at sea.

You realize, Noah,
for a sloth,

just how important
sleeping is?
Both night
and day!
In fact,
I'd say
...
zzzzzzz

Judith Nicholls

37

Happy Dogday

Today –
Is our dog's birthday.

It's Happydogdayday.
Sixteen years of panting
And sixteen years of play.

Sixteen years of dogtime.
Sixteen years of barks
– eating smelly dog food
And making muddy marks.

It's a hundred years of our time
It's a hundred human years
– of digging in the garden
And scratching itchy ears.

A hundred years of living rooms
(he never goes upstairs)
and dropping hairy whiskers
And being pushed off chairs...

It's a hundred years of being with us
A hundred years of Dad...
And a hundred of my sister
(that must be really bad!)

So:

No wonder he looks really old
No wonder he is grey
And cannot hear
Or jump
Or catch
Or even run away...
No wonder that he sleeps all day
No wonder that he's fat
And only dreams of catching thin
And chasing neighbours' cats...

So fight your fights
In dogdream nights
Deep within your bed...

today's your day
and we all say...

Happy Birthday FRED!

Peter Dixon

Lion

Great rag bag
jumble headed thing
shakes its mane
in a yawn that turns to anger,
teeth picked out like stalactites
in some vast cave
bone grinders, flesh rippers
hyena bringers, jackal callers
and huge paws
the size of death
clamp down on antelope,
later, sleeping through the night
each star a lion
flung with pride across a sky
black as a roaring mouth
lion dreams of open spaces
dreams the smell of freedom.

David Harmer

Caterpillar v Snail

Starts fast
legs ache...
Cabbage leaf,
quick break!
Eat much,
warm sun...
Snail's passed,
SNAIL WON!

One foot
starts slow.
Long way.
Food? No!
Keep on,
snail's pace.
Slowcoach
WINS RACE!

Judith Nicholls

39

Sick as a Parrot

This parrot is not a nice bird,
It is spiteful and moody and red.
Its eyes are hot and flash a lot
In its bird-brained little head.

This parrot is not a pretty bird,
Its feathers are dusty and sad,
Its tail is green without any sheen
And its dandruff is awfully bad.

This parrot is not entertaining,
Doesn't sing, doesn't dance, doesn't speak.
It just sits and stares and mutters and glares
And hammers its perch with its beak.

This parrot belonged to Grandad,
It chattered all day by his side,
It used to recite Old King Cole every night
But it's dumbstruck since Grandad has died.

Shelagh McGee

The Codfish

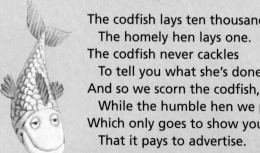

The codfish lays ten thousand eggs,
   The homely hen lays one.
The codfish never cackles
   To tell you what she's done.
And so we scorn the codfish,
   While the humble hen we prize,
Which only goes to show you
   That it pays to advertise.

Anon

My Dear Pet

My baby rhino
is a playful little mite.
I ask her to stamp on my pastry dough
with her round flat foot.
Then I fill the footprint
with apples and raisins and cinnamon
and we have a party
with Hawaiian Punch
and apple pie covered in cream.
I know everyone boasts
about their singing turtles
and dancing stick insects
like they were hot stuff.
I don't care
because I've got a proud feeling
about my rhino.
So do you want to know her name?
I say to her, "Rosie, sit still
and stop trotting through the park –
these children want to see
what an ideal rhino you are."
She tickles me with her velvet ears
when I'm grumpy.
That's when she thinks
I'm her human pet.

Julie O'Callaghan

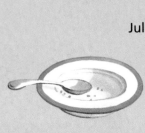

News of the Python

Leopards tussled.
Monkeys flew.
The python breathed.

Water bubbled.
Storm-gusts grew.
The python breathed.

Ice-cream tumbled.
Paper blew.
The python breathed.

Easter Sunday
At the zoo:
The python breathed.

Libby Houston

Bear Clothes

A Polar Bear's coat
buttons up to his throat
to keep out the cold
and snow.

A Polar Bear's scarf
would make you laugh
for he ties it up
in a bow.

A Polar Bear's boots
are useful on routes
for making his insides
glow.

But when it is hot
he wears what he's got,
a bare Bear from head
to toe.

Pie Corbett

Animals in the Zoo Are Like People

I liked the cheeky chimpanzee –
my brother said it looked like me.

So I replied, "Your head's the shape
of that old, big old, fat old ape!"

He said, "Just look at that baboon –
it's got a face like Auntie June!!"

We stood right by the lion's cage:
it roared like Dad does in a rage,

and then it lay down in a heap
like Dad does when he goes to sleep.

And Mum is like a kangaroo –
her apron's got a pocket too.

We saw a hippopotamus.
(Gran said to Grandad, "Looks like us!")

But tell me, out of every creature,
which was the one that looked like teacher?

And lastly, out of all the zoo,
which was the one that looked like YOU?

Charles Thomson

Fishbones Dreaming

Fishbones lay in the smelly bin.
He was a head, a backbone and a tail.
Soon the cats would be in for him.

He didn't like to be this way.
He shut his eyes and dreamed back.

Back to when he was fat, and hot on a plate.
Beside green beans, with lemon juice
squeezed on him. And a man
with a knife and fork raised, about to eat him.

He didn't like to be this way.
He shut his eyes and dreamed back.

Back to when he was squirming in a net,
with thousands of other fish, on the deck of a boat.
And the rain falling wasn't wet enough to breathe in.

He didn't like to be this way.
He shut his eyes and dreamed back.

Back to when he was darting through the sea,
past crabs and jellyfish, and others like himself.
Or surfacing to jump for flies
and feel the sun on his face.

He liked to be this way.
He dreamed hard to try and stay there.

Matthew Sweeney

44

Watercat

Our cat used to like water.
If Dad set up the sprinkler
he'd come in wet through
from leaping after
fountains in the air;

and he liked the aquarium,
would balance on the rim
trying to hook fishes,
until one day he fell in
and had to be rescued.

He lost interest then.
When he notices now
the flash of fish at play
he settles down on the rug,
facing the other way.

Irene Rawnsley

Song-Thrush

Slug-slayer, snail-snatcher,
soprano turned percussionist,
mad drummer of the rock;
now executioner,
still centre-stage,
beats out her dizzy solo
on execution block.

Judith Nicholls

45

Dog's Life

I don't like being me sometimes
      slumped here
on the carpet, cocking my ears
      every time
someone shuffles or shifts their feet
      thinking
could be I'm going walkies or getting grub
      or allowed
to see if the cat's left more than a smell
      on her plate.
She's never refused, that cat! Sometimes
      I find myself

dreaming – twitching my fur, my ears – of
      being just
say *half* as canny as her, with her pert miaow,
      her cheeky tail
flaunting! These people sprawled
      in armchairs
gawping at telly, why don't they play ball
      with me
or enjoy a good nose-licking, eh?

Matt Simpson

If You Should Meet a Crocodile

If you should meet a crocodile,
  Don't take a stick and poke him;
Ignore the welcome in his smile,
  Be careful not to stroke him.

For as he sleeps upon the Nile,
  He thinner gets and thinner;
And whene'er you meet a crocod
  He's ready for his dinner.

Anon

Dancing the Anaconda

A n a c o n d a
starts to "Conga!" through a jungle (not the Congo).
Twisting round, along, then round, branch and
bough are danced around;
so smooth, except a bulge or two, where a
not-so-quick-step bird (or beast) or two, groove
to a graver tune.
A n a c o n d a
hokey-cokeys quite a few.

A n a c o n d a
growing longer.
Rivers offer no restriction to choreography's
constriction; the list of practised tactics
includes ballet aquatic.
"Come, we conga like a conger to apocalypso frogs,
or maybe rumba numbers that bop Orinoco hogs."

If you hear nocturnal rocking, when snake
charmers should be curling tight, it could be
A n a c o n d a
sleepwaltzing through those tango-tangled
forests of the night.

"Excuse me," for a danceclass treat, as
F   r   e   d
and
G i n g e r
A n a c o n d a
meet.
(They never tread on one another's feet.)

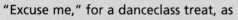

Mike Johnson

47

Alligator in the Zoo

A long slow line of leather
green and brown, all but dead.

A razor smile of icy teeth
a broad corrugated back

as tough as bark, like tree trunk
half-submerged by water.

Above the jaws set like traps
fathers dangle their babies' legs.

Dragon breath is smouldering
bubbling up from the snout.

One dropped shoe or careless kick
one brief sag of aching arms

and that huge mouth
will split apart like a flick-knife

snap the prey up
like a trout traps a fly.

David Harmer

48

The Purpose of Keeping a Tortoise

A tortoise
is not a pet I long to keep.
In Summer?
All he does is eat and crawl.
In Winter?
Hide and sleep!

Judith Nicholls

Natty Bats

weird world of hi-fi echoes
they flittermouse around

fishing with their ultra-ears
for food in nets of sound

well-fed suspended from their toes

natty bats sleep upside-down!

Mike Johnson

The Ptarmigan

The ptarmigan is strange,
As strange as he can be;
Never sits on the ptelephone poles
Or roosts upon a ptree.
And the way he ptakes pto spelling
Is the strangest thing pto me.

Anon

The Dragon

Underneath our teapot stand,
in a small, compacted world
of dry dropped tealeaves,
a sulky dragon sleeps.

He wakens every once a while
for maidens from the biscuit tin
to bring him Current Crisp crumbs
or broken Garibaldis.

How he longs to see a shining knight
ride into his lonely kingdom,
with a coloured shield and flashing sword,
to remind him of the old days.

I would go and play with him
and cheer his melancholy,
and I would help the maidens fair
carry their gifts to his castle, but

I'm not supposed to know he's there.

Robin Mellor

There Was a Small Maiden Named Maggie

There was a small maiden named Maggie,
Whose dog was enormous and shaggy;
The front end of him
Looked vicious and grim –
But the tail end was friendly and waggy.

Anon

The Whalig and His Ele-Friend

Rasher the pig met Cutlet the calf
not knowing how lucky they were
        by half.

Of Rasher, his rear was rounded and pink,
with flickers of blotches like blotted black ink,
that came to an end in a question-mark tail.
The question was, was he a pig or a whale?
For Rasher, up front, was really a teaser –

no trotters, no snout, and he spouted a geyser
from in-between where his ears should have sprung.
This *whalig*, to market, should never have come
for there wasn't a farmer, nor butcher, would buy
as *whaligs* won't breed and *whaligs* won't fry!

But Rasher got shot in a photograph
not knowing how lucky he was
        by half.

Now Cutlet the calf had sugar brown eyes,
a wet leather nose and ears twice the size
of her sandpaper tongue that sucked, as a thumb,
(what else can a calf do when taken from Mum?)
the end of her tail which was whippy and grey

till, ropy and wet, it started to fray
and straggle in strands down her baggy back end.
Cutlet, the calf, *whalig*'s strange *ele-friend*,
was suitable neither for veal nor for hunting
which went in her favour – there had to be something!

So Cutlet and Rasher had the last laugh
not knowing how lucky they were
        by half.
                Gina Douthwaite

Cat

Cat's sneaky,
leaps onto my lap
with sudden claws
like nettle stings.

And now she is
tucking herself away –
O so tidily – right down to
her Chinese eyes.

Purrs like a lawnmower...
Yes, but her ears, her ears
are watching something

that hops and twitters
worm-hungry,
among the wet petunias.

Matt Simpson

The Pelican

What a wonderful beast is the Pelican!
Whose bill can hold more than his belican.
  He can take in his beak
  Enough food for a week –
    And I'm damned
    if I know
      how the helican.

Anon

52

My Dog

My dog belongs to no known breed,
A bit of this and that.
His head looks like a small haystack
He's lazy, smelly, fat.

If I say, "Sit!" he walks away.
When I throw stick or ball
He flops down in the grass as if
He had no legs at all,

And looks at me with eyes that say,
"You threw the thing, not me.
You want it back, then get it back.
Fair's fair, you must agree."

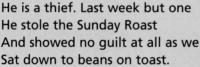

He is a thief. Last week but one
He stole the Sunday Roast
And showed no guilt at all as we
Sat down to beans on toast.

The only time I saw him run –
And he went like a flash –
Was when a mugger in the park
Tried to steal my cash.

My loyal, brave companion flew
Like a missile to the gate
And didn't stop till safely home.
He left me to my fate.

And would I swap him for a dog
Obedient, clean and good,
An honest, faithful, lively chap?
Oh boy, I would! I would!

Vernon Scannell

53

The Ballad of Unicorn Isle

Once upon a faraway time
Before the clocks had learned to chime
When every river spoke in rhyme,
Once upon a time...

Once within a distant land
Where mountains hadn't heard of man
Where dolphins played and bluebirds sang,
Once within a land...

Then and there in echoing light
Where gold was day and silver night
Lived unicorns of purest black and white,
There in echoing light.

One shining day in shimmering glade
The seer had come to speak, they said:
An ancient one with eyes of jade,
One shimmering, shining day.

"I saw the future faraway –
Hearken, friends, to what I say!
I saw grey night and I saw grey day
In the future far away.

I saw the pale two-legged beast
Rise up from west, rise up from east
And slay our kind for fun and feast,
The pale two-legged beast.

It hunted down the unicorn;
It cut off head, it cut off horn
Or stole our foals as they were born
And caged the noble unicorn."

54

Once upon a desperate hour
In the shadow of the great Moonflower
They made a pact to use their power,
Upon a desperate hour.

So faded they from human sight
Though wild geese see them from their flight
And children dream of them at night,
Invisible to human sight.

... Once within a faraway land
Where unicorns first heard of man
Where hotels rise and tourists tan,
Once within a land...

Trevor Millum

Cecil and the Widow

Cecil the spider –
a creepy-crawler –
Met his beloved,
called Maude the Mauler.

His little bug eyes
popped out as he spied her,
While she licked her lips
all wet with saliva.

Cecil once was
a gigolo spider,
But he's now turned into
the dinner inside her.

Mistreat her; scorn her;
abuse her; deride her –
But NEVER cuddle up
to a Black Widow Spider.

Roger Tulk

Elephants

If a hundred elephants
tried to board a bus
would the driver
make a fuss?

And if fifty elephants
came all together
to do their shopping at Tesco
would it cause
a fiasco?

And if twenty elephants
came one morning
to school
with books in their trunks
would the teacher
keep her cool?

And if one
very little elephant,
smaller than all the rest
wanted to be my friend
for just one day
would my mum
let him stay?

Irene Rawnsley

Sloth

There's a three-toed sloth in my apple tree:
I'm staring at him and he's staring at me;
There's all kinds of things that I want to ask,
But I fear that it might be a very long task,
'Cos a three-toed sloth, as you probably know,
Is incredibly wise – *but incredibly slow.*

(So
Stop and think about it.

*That's good, thinks the sloth,
I like people who stop
to think about things*.)

"I'd like to ask, if you have the time,
Of all the apple trees, why choose mine?"

I stood for an hour and I gazed at the sky;
Then the sloth just winked one languid eye,
as if to say – *When you go hanging from trees,
You can pick on any old tree you please.*

I stood for an hour and I gazed at the sun,
Then I said to the sloth – "Now would it be fun
To come on inside and have some tea?"
But the three-toed sloth didn't answer me.

I stood for an hour and I gazed at a cloud,
Till at last I thought a thought out loud
and I said – "Is it better to hang and sway
from an apple-tree branch or to sleep all day?"

He hung and he swayed, that three-toed sloth,
Then he smiled very slowly and answered: *Both!*

Tony Charles

57

Ten Dancing Dinosaurs

Ten dancing dinosaurs in a chorus line
One fell and split her skirt, then there were nine.

Nine dancing dinosaurs at a village fête
One was raffled as a prize, then there were eight.

Eight dancing dinosaurs on a pier in Devon
One fell overboard, then there were seven.

Seven dancing dinosaurs performing magic tricks
One did a vanishing act, then there were six.

Six dancing dinosaurs learning how to jive
One got twisted in a knot, then there were five.

Five dancing dinosaurs gyrating on the floor
One crashed through the floorboards, then there were four.

Four dancing dinosaurs waltzing in the sea
A mermaid kidnapped one, then there were three.

Three dancing dinosaurs head-banging in a zoo
One knocked himself out, then there were two.

Two dancing dinosaurs rocking round the sun
One collapsed from sunstroke, then there was one.

One dancing dinosaur hijacked a plane
Flew off to Alaska and was never seen again!

John Foster

The Car Park Cat

```
        △                  K
    E C                  R C
    H A                  A A
    T R                  P T
```

Car bonnet cat
keeping warm, car bonnet cat
with crocodile yawn, stares from his sand-
peppered forest of fluff, segment-of-lemon eyes warning,
ENOUGH! Just draw back that hand, retreat, *GO AWAY!*
and his claws flex a tune to say: I won't play but I'll spit
like the sea whipped wild in a gale, hump up like a wave,
flick a forked lightning tail, lash out and scratch at
your lobster-pink face, for no one, *but no one*,
removes from this place, car bonnet cat
keeping warm, car bonnet cat
by the name of
STORM.

Gina Douthwaite

Goldfish Lament

I'm a goldfish
a cold fish,
a put-me-in-a-bowl fish –
where am I going to go?

I'd like to be an old fish
I've told fish,
but now that I'm a sold fish
I fear that won't be so.

Judith Nicholls

Hammy's House

Jane next door
has gone to Spain;
they wouldn't let her
take a hamster on the plane
so we're looking after him.

But the cage she brought
was cramped and small;
he scarcely had room
to move at all,
just a wheel, a dish and straw.

Dad said,
"He's got no room to play!
This hamster's
supposed to be on holiday.
Let's give him a surprise!"

He searched the garage
that very day
for the old doll's house
we'd thrown away,
mended the broken hinges,

put nuts inside,
screwed the wheel in place,
found fresh straw
for his sleeping space,
then popped him through the door.

Now he's busy
arranging his nest,
sorting his nuts out,
finding the best
to store in his bedroom,

working out on the wheel
of his gymnasium;
he'll not want to go back
when Jane comes home.
Maybe she'll let us keep him.

Irene Rawnsley

There Wasn't a Shark at London Zoo

We saw a monkey coloured blue
but there wasn't a shark at London Zoo.

We saw the gorillas do kung fu
but there wasn't a shark at London Zoo.

We saw a leap-frogging kangaroo
but there wasn't a shark at London Zoo.

We saw some pigs (and what a pooh!)
but there wasn't a shark at London Zoo.

There were elephants there and lions too
but there wasn't a shark at London Zoo.

There were antelopes and a caribou
but there wasn't a shark at London Zoo.

We even joined a massive queue
but there wasn't a shark at London Zoo.

Question

Is it really, really, really true
that there isn't a shark at London Zoo?*

*"Oh no, there isn't a shark – we've got a
dogfish," I was told. I wonder if a dogfish
can bark underwater?

Charles Thomson

61

The Camel's Hump

What's in the hump's a mystery
unparalleled in history.
Some say it's there for food and so on –
what evidence have they to go on?
I think it's like an empty tin
which he keeps bits and pieces in
(and how does a camel keep up his hump?
He blows it up with a bicycle pump!)

The proof for this is quite immense
if we apply some common sense,
so first let's answer this enquiry –
where does a camel keep his diary?
Not in a drawer, or on a rack
but tucked up safely on his back
(and how does a camel keep up his hump?
He blows it up with a bicycle pump!)

Where does he store away utensils?
Where does he put his pen and pencils?
Where does he keep his watch all night?
They're hidden safely out of sight,
not in a bag or plastic sack
but in the bump upon his back.
(and how does a camel keep up his hump?
He blows it up with a bicycle pump!)

Charles Thomson

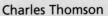

Spider

Every morning at my sink
a spider crawls down for a drink.
She abseils from the window-sill
then folds up, keeping very still
until she thinks I've gone away
then
one leg,
two legs,
feel their way.
They prod, they probe,
legs *three*
and *four*
join in the fun. Then even more!
Legs *five*
and *six*
extend and lift
hydraulically – she tilts a bit
till hairy members
seven
and *eight*
receive their message, "ACTIVATE".
And so, across the soapy trickle,
she *flits*! – black threads of silky tickle –
till tidal waves, tipped from the bowl,
send her whirlpooling down the hole

* * * * * *

then
one leg,
two legs,
feel their way...

Gina Douthwaite

Wanted – a Witch's Cat

Wanted – a witch's cat.
Must have vigour and spite,
Be expert at hissing,
And good in a fight,
And have balance and poise
On a broomstick at night.

Wanted – a witch's cat.
Must have hypnotic eyes
To tantalize victims
And mesmerize spies,
And be an adept
At scanning the skies.

Wanted – a witch's cat.
With a sly, cunning smile,
A knowledge of spells
And a good deal of guile,
With a fairly hot temper
And plenty of bile.

Wanted – a witch's cat.
Who's not afraid to fly,
For a cat with strong nerves
The salary's high.
Wanted – a witch's cat;
Only the best need apply.

Shelagh McGee

The Mouse and the Xmas Tree

The mouse ran up the Xmas tree
   hey ho, hey ho,
through a well-lit, uphill forest
   that wasn't there before
and he thought: all these bells
and stars, and deer, and dwarves
   are brill and honey-dandy
and I'll nibble some to prove it
but as I alone can climb the tree
   I am still the best.

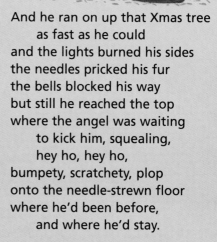

And through the tree's green needles
   came the mouse's song:
   Hey ho, hey ho,
I'm fed up with the floor.
I'm even more bored
   with the world behind
     the skirting-board.
I like this stood-up wood.

And he ran on up that Xmas tree
   as fast as he could
and the lights burned his sides
the needles pricked his fur
the bells blocked his way
but still he reached the top
where the angel was waiting
   to kick him, squealing,
   hey ho, hey ho,
bumpety, scratchety, plop
onto the needle-strewn floor
where he'd been before,
   and where he'd stay.

Matthew Sweeney

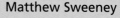

Tell Me It Isn't

Try not to stare
But tell me – that shadow there
With its head in the air
Isn't a bear...
There isn't a bear
Come out of its lair
At the top of the stair,
IS there??

Take care how you speak,
But – tell me, that creak,
It isn't the creak of the freak,
The flying freak
With the crooked beak
About to sneak
Up from behind,
IS it??

Tell me that sound
Isn't the sound of the hound,
The red-eyed hound
Creeping around
Dribbling and crunching
The bones it found
About to leap with one bound
On my back!
(It isn't, is it?)

Tell me – the movement I saw
Behind the door...
It wasn't a paw
It wasn't a claw
It wasn't the Beast
About to roar
And pounce and gnaw – WAS IT?

Yes, I know you told me before
But I'm still not sure,
So... tell me *once* more.

Trevor Millum

The Ancient Horrors

I met an ancient Vampire once
whilst ambling on the heath:
the bloodbank had to give him blood –
he'd lost his new false teeth.

I met an ancient Hagwitch once:
her home help came each day
to bring her beetle juice and toast
with frogs' legs on a tray.

I met an ancient Werewolf once
who said, "You'll do for tea,"
but he was in a wheelchair, so
he didn't frighten me.

I met an ancient Ghostie once
who seemed quite out of breath;
he tried to make a moaning sound
and coughed himself to death.

I met an ancient Monster once
who lived around Loch Ness,
but she was only one foot high
(she'd shrunk with age I guess).

I met an ancient Zombie once:
he sent me into fits,
for when he went to grab my arm
he promptly fell to bits.

Marian Swinger/Charles Thomson

The Hoover Spook

A naughty spook named Norman Head
sneaked in and hid beneath a bed.

Then, while the owners dozed inside,
he lurked amidst the dust and spied

until a sleepy let hung out,
grabbed hold with an excited shout

and caused the couple so much fright
their hair went absolutely white.

Next day the trembling couple said,
"Let's vacuum underneath the bed.

If anything is hiding there
we'll give it an almighty scare."

Next moment Norman gave a wail
to find himself amidst a gale,

he clung in panic to a spring,
he lost his grasp, there was a PING!

With bulging eyes and frenzied shout
he vanished up the vacuum spout.

A prisoner in the Hoover bag
with spiders, dust and half a fag,

poor Norman brooded hard and long
on making the machine go wrong.

That night the Hoover gave a roar
and spread its contents on the floor.

Encouraged by this great success
in manufacturing a mess

(on which a spook's good name depends)
he notified his ghostly friends,

"Don't waste your time beneath a bed –
frequent a Hoover bag instead."

So if your Hoover splurts out dust,
don't look inside unless you must.

It's almost certain, if you do,
a horrid spook will yell out "BOO!!!"

Marian Swinger/
Charles Thomson

Willy Was a Wizard

Willy was a Wizard
who could never spell it right:
tried to fix a thunderstorm –
got the sun at night;
tried to paint his top hat black –
ended up with white;
couldn't even scare a flea
or give a mouse a fright;
SPELLS FOR ALL, the notice said,
but that was there in spite
of Willy being a Wizard
who couldn't get it right!

Judith Nicholls

Mary Celeste

On the Atlantic Ocean
The light winds blow
And the abandoned ship
Tacks crazily to and fro.

Safe and sound,
The ship sails on;
Only the lifeboat
And people are gone.

One of the hatches
Is lying open
But the cargo's intact
And nothing's missing or broken.

No sign why the crew,
The captain, his child and wife
Should suddenly panic
And flee for dear life.

No signs of a struggle to be seen,
But a letter left half-written
And a reel of cotton and a thimble
In place on the sewing machine.

On the Atlantic Ocean
The light winds blow
And the abandoned ship
Tacks crazily to and fro.

Tins of food seized from the store,
But the captain's watch on its hook
Pipes left and tobacco
And jewels and trinkets in a drawer.

Stanley Cook

70

The Room Went Cold

The room went cold
and I felt something
like a sticky hand
creep along my neck
and down my spine.

It trickled down my leg
stroked my foot
then slid off my toe
and onto the floor.

I stared with one eye
I stared with two eyes
I got my magnifying glass
and my dad's binoculars
and my sister's ruler
and the kitchen scales

so I could see it
measure it
weigh it

but there was

nothing to see

nothing to measure

nothing to weigh

nothing to be
frightened of

was there?

Sue Stewart

Fearless

Ghosts and foul ghoulies
I can withstand;
skeletons, witches,
I'd take by the hand.
A poltergeist's welcome,
a dragon is grand
BUT...

Who'll move the spider?

Dinosaurs, Krakens –
such friendly ways!
Octopus, jellyfish,
Martians from space.
The Centaur, a phoenix
I'd look in the face
BUT...

Who'll move the spider?

Judith Nicholls

71

What's There?

Raging, crazily, round the roof
as though in torture from a tooth
this uninvited guest gyrates,
cracks creaking beams, whips under slates,
prises open trapdoor jaws,
pads across cold bedroom floors,
rattles handles,
battles
with doors,

hides in curtains, whines and s-i-g-h-s,
traces flesh with fingers of ice,
SCREAMS down chimneys, *startling* flames.
Hear breathless voices wailing names?
hoaxing, coaxing from the stair,
calling cats who bristle hair,
cower and yowl
at what – ?
What's there

raging, crazily, round the roof?

They say they know – but where's the proof?

Gina Douthwaite

72

Dracula's Complaint

You'd look poorly, you'd look pale
Skin all deathly shades of grey
You'd look sickly, you'd look frail
Stuck in a coffin in a grave all day.

Go for a shave but I can't see my face
Spend half my life dressed up as a bat
Living all my days at a subnormal pace
With these enormous teeth, who needs that?

Night after night I ride my bike
Looking around for a bite to eat
Living in a graveyard isn't what I like
The neighbours howl, their breath's not sweet.

I'm bored stiff, it's a pain in the neck
Living in the ground, cold and damp
I'm turning into a Transylvanian wreck
My whole life needs a thorough re-vamp.

I look in the paper, read the small ads
I need a new job, need a fresh start
I want to escape the curse of the Vlads
Try to do that with a stake through your heart.

David Harmer

Grandma's Dream

This is the dream that Grandma saw.
The dream came back year after year

Always the same – like a film – she said:
She was going along a country road,

Along the road and in at the gates
(Horses' heads on the weather-worn posts),

In at the gates and down the drive
(A yellow tower from a dark grove),

Down the drive and up to the door
(Tracks in the gravel like a turning car's

But no car nor cart nor carriage now),
By the shallow steps in the glaring view

Of thirty-five windows (blank as water
In an old canal in a summer shadow)

And over the threshold and into the hall
(From the gilded ceiling the air hung still).

No one challenged her, no voice spoke,
No cough, no footstep, rustle nor click.

Corkscrew pillars of clouded marble –
Between them stood a massive table

Covered, in all that solemn splendour,
With rubbish – more than she ever remembered –

Like screwed-up papers grey with grease,
Green-flecked bread with a half-chewed slice,

Snot-glued tissues, slimy skin,
Curd-smeared bottles and a fallen beam,

Tea-bags, coke cans – Grandma stared.
Beyond the hearth a shadow stirred:

A dark arched door began to open
For a girl with a tray, in a long apron.

The girl saw Grandma in her dream,
Dropped the tray with a wild scream
And flung her apron up over her face –

She always woke at the same place.

Grandma's dream. Or was Grandma a ghost
For a real girl somewhere in a real house?

Libby Houston

Faith

There was a young lady of Ryde,
Who was carried too far by the tide;
    A man-eating shark
    Said: "How's this for a lark?
I knew that the Lord would provide.

Anon

Assembly

I don't want to see any racing in the corridor,
a gentle glide's what we expect in here;
not that I mind a little heavy-handed fear
but you high spirits must slow down.

And I've had complaints that some of you
slip out at playtime. Let it be quite clear
that you stay in the graveyard till you hear
the bell. The chippy's out of bounds,
so is the sweetshop and your other favourite haunts.
I'll stop your little fun and groans:
there'll be a year's detention in the dungeon
for anyone caught chewing anything but bones.

And we'll have no more silly tricks with slamming doors,
at your age you should be walking through the walls.
And it isn't nice to use your loose heads as footballs
or vanish when you're being spoken to.

And finally, I really must remind you
that moans are not allowed before midnight
especially near the staff-room. It's impolite
and disturbs the creatures – I mean teachers –
resting in despair and mournful gloom.
You there – stop wriggling in your coffin, I can't
bear to see a scruffy ghost –
put your face back where it was this instant
or you won't get to go howling at the moon.

76

Class Three, instead of double Shrieking
you'll do Terminal Disease with Dr. Cyst;
Class Two stays here for Creepy Sneaking.
The rest of you can go. School dismissed.

Dave Calder

What My Father Said

"Great Aunt Alice used to live
in a coffin,"
my father said,
"But was she dead?"
I asked,
"Oh no," he replied,
"At least, I don't think so."

"Old Uncle Jerome never had
a home,"
my father said,
"But used to wander
the streets alone with
a sack on his head.
He's dead."

"Your mother's brother,"
my father said,
"Had a bit of bother with
a sliced loaf of bread."
"Yes?" I asked,
"Yes," my father said.

My father said
"Just look at the time.
Come on,
up the wooden hill
it's just a short climb.
Off you go to bed."

But I can't sleep
and I'm thinking still,
should I believe
what my father said?

Robin Mellor

Why Are We Hiding?

Why are we hiding in here?
Why are we hiding in here?
What's up? What's there? What makes you stare?
Why are we hiding in here?

Why are we hiding in here?
Is it that breathing noise coming near –
Is that the thing I've got to fear?

Why are we hiding in here?
Is it that shape that's begun to appear –
Is that the thing I've got to fear?

Why are we hiding in here?
Is it that outline becoming clear –
Is that the thing I've got to fear?

DON'T tell me that there's nothing to fear
I KNOW there's something coming near
And NOTHING you say will make it disappear
OH – WHY are we hiding in here?

Trevor Millum

Creepy

Ghosts and goblins don't strike me as creepy –
If anything, they bore me and make me feel sleepy.
I know they're not real – more like a bad dream.
It's the *real* Creepy-Crawlies that make *me* scream!

Gavin Ewart

The Ghost

You may have to wait for hours
For a bus or a train
Or wait the whole of the year
For Christmas to come again.

But the hundreds of years
The ghost had to wait
Have almost worn him away
And he is thin and his voice is faint.

He has worn out the home he had
When once he was alive
And only a few battered ruins
From the walls of his castle survive.

He has grown as pale
As a gleam of moonlight
Coming through a gap in the curtains
As the old church clock strikes midnight.

Don't try to seize him –
He is thin as a shadow;
Listen carefully –
His voice is faint as an echo.

He is so worn out
You hardly know he is there
When he passes you by
In a gust of ice-cold air.

Stanley Cook

Camping Out

Can we sleep out in the tent, Dad?
Go on, just him and me!
It's a full moon,
not a cloud in sight!
We'll be quiet as
mice when the cat's about –
oh, *please* let us stay the night?

*You can pitch your tent down
    the garden
by the lilac, or just behind;
but mind you're in by midnight
if you're going to change your
mind.
The key will be out till twelve,
but not a second more.
I don't want prowlers after that –
at twelve I lock the door!*

Great Dad!
We'll be out till morning –
you've never let us before!
We'll fetch all we need
before it's dark
then you can lock your door.

*The key will be out till twelve,
I said, but not a second more!*

Now what do we need?
Water, jug, toothpaste, mug
towel, rug,
toothbrush
    ...

*Since when were you so keen
on keeping clean?*

You can't camp out down
    the Amazon
without the proper gear.
We could be here a year,
exploring dark Brazil
until – who knows?

*All right, a torch then,
I suppose. Sleeping bags.
Pillows?*

There's no room.
Mosquito nets come first,
and books to read
by torch or moon.
Pencils, notebooks.
Sweaters – two at least.
And don't forget the
    midnight feast!

*What do explorers eat?
Will crisps and apples do,
with peanut-butter sandwiches,
bananas, orange juice,
and baked beans for the stew?*

They'll do!
    ...

I wish we'd brought a pillow.
It's really dark.
I thought you said no cloud?
Should we close the flap –
to keep mosquitoes out, I mean?

Or leopards!

...and to keep us warm.
There goes that flash again.
The air feels heavy.
P'rhaps a jungle storm?
Listen!
Can you hear – a breeze?
Something's rustling,
quickly, *freeze!*

Could it be
some deadly snake,
uncoiling for...

For goodness sake,
it's only trees!
Why are we whispering?

Oh, look!
What IS that shadow up above?
I'm sure I saw it move!

It's nothing,
just the lilac.
Or some bat or owl
out on the prowl
for supper too.

TOOWHIT, TOOWHOO!

No need to jump,
it's nearer me than you!

I didn't jump!
What time is it,
only five to midnight?
Just wondered.
Thought it might be more.

I DON'T WANT PROWLERS AFTER THAT,
AT TWELVE I LOCK THE DOOR!...

Aren't you cold?
I wish we'd brought more blankets,
the jungle's not so hot
when sun's gone down;
we didn't think of that.

Not cold, just hungry.
It's great out here,
but as for food –
we should have brought much more.
Explorers need their sustenance.
Another time, we'll plan it better...

But meantime,
RACE YOU TO THE DOOR!

Judith Nicholls

81

Under the Bedclothes

What is it walking outside in the dark?
Is it the ghost of poor Mollie Park,
who lived all alone with the spiders and rats?
– *Cover your ears and pretend it's just cats!*

What is it tapping the window so gently?
Is it the ghost of poor Johnny Bentley,
Who fell off a cliff when no one was near?
– *Cover your ears and pretend you can't hear!*

What is it dripping downstairs in the kitchen?
Is it the ghost of poor Billy Ditchen,
Who drowned with his dog in the cold grey stream?
– *Cover your ears and pretend it's a dream!*

What is it creaking upstairs so slowly?
Is it the ghost of poor Mollie Coley,
With old tattered clothing and twigs in her hair?
– *Cover your ears and pretend she's not there!*

What is it opening the bedroom door
And moving so softly across the floor?
– *Cover your ears, and close your eyes tight,
And just hope that it's Mum come to see you're all right!*

Tony Charles

82

Who's Afraid?

Do I have to go haunting tonight?
The children might give me a fright.
It's dark in that house.
I might meet a mouse.
Do I have to go haunting tonight?

I don't like the way they scream out,
When they see me skulking about.
I'd much rather stay here,
Where there's nothing to fear.
Do I have to go haunting tonight?

John Foster

The Follower

Hiding like a tree cat
in a dappled cave of leaves,
watching like a kestrel
soaring high above the eaves,

Stalking as a grey wolf
through the misty heather,
stealthy as a wily fox
scenting fur or feather,

Padding close as tigers
to the edges of your mind,
whose the footsteps following?

Dare you look behind?

Irene Rawnsley

83

The Gloom

What waits?
Up the dark alley,
Knife sharp and glinting,
Cooking pot ready.

What lives?
Inside the chimney,
Moaning and howling,
Calling down thunder.

THE GLOOM!

What hides?
Under the wardrobe,
Licking its fat chops,
Grabbing at ankles.

What moves?
Invisibly through you,
Creaking the floorboards,
Making you shudder.

THE GLOOM!

What haunts?
Old empty houses,
Overgrown graveyards,
Your very worst dream.

But what runs?
When you make up a poem,
Blow a loud raspberry
Then sing a daft song.

THE GLOOM!

Kevin McCann

Cooked

A careless old cook of Saltash
In her second-hand car had a crash;
    She drove through a wall,
    House, garden and all,
And ended up Banger-and-Mash.

Anon

Silas Scale's Piano

Silas Scale left in his will
an instrument that can't keep still.

With phantom fingers on the keys
it strikes out quavers, semibreves,
and renders rondos, unrequested.

Such mechanism must be tested!
Silas Scale's piano's front

was purposely removed to hunt
for tiny paw marks in the dust –
the answer to the mystery must

be found in mice abseiling wires,
or twanging chords to tune up choirs

for mousical productions of
Shaketail's "Cheese – The Food We Love".
...No Phily-monic escapades

nor older-rodent matinées
had taken place, which quite perturbed –

dust lay too deep and undisturbed
for mousy-style participation.
No hand had they. What implication?

Scale's piano held no clue yet
yesterday it played a duet

enchanting all who heard this vital,
truly spirited recital
from Silas Scale's piano.

Gina Douthwaite

85

Dusk Jockey

Good evening, everyone.
Let me remind you who I am.
I am not your favourite man.
You've never seen me but you know my voice.
The tunes I play make none of you rejoice:
They're what you'd call decidedly unpop
The only charts that they'd be sure to top
Would be a list of sounds you most detest.
Now and then I bring along a guest
To give my programme added interest:
I had a vampire in the studio
No longer than half-an-hour ago
But he was thirsty and he had to go.
He says he hopes he'll visit some of you
For one quick drink before the night is through.
If you're anaemic you can sleep quite tight
Except a news flash filtered through last night:
A madman has infected all supplies
Of water everywhere. Perhaps all lies,
But I wouldn't bet on it if I were you.
And now a card from Mr Pettigrew
Who says he's looking forward keenly to
The funeral of Mrs Pettigrew.
Some music now for Mrs Thumb and Tom –
The Zombies' March and Lepers' Chorus from
An opera whose title slips my mind.

And then I've got to go, before the blind
Of total night comes down. But don't believe I'm through:
Dusk is the time I find most work to do.
I've got to groom my mount while there's still light;
I'll ride my mare into your sleep tonight.

Vernon Scannell

Spider Night

Darkness
has too many legs,
walks high and silently
across wide spaces
into everywhere;

spreads hands
like spider webs
across your garden,
your house,
your room;

watches
through the long night
with unsleeping
spiders' eyes;

hears you breathing.

Irene Rawnsley

Ode to a Nightingown

The sound disturbed the peaceful night,
a song we could not recognise.
We looked out at star-freckled skies;
No living creature met our sight.

It sounded like the slap of waves,
Yet somehow not a liquid sound,
More like the wind that prowls around
And through a forest's leafy caves.

But there were neither waves nor trees
Within a score of miles from where
We looked across the little square
Of our backyard and saw the frieze

Of roofs and chimneys and the frail
Scaffolding of aerials;
And then again, like wooden bells
Or distant speech of flapping sail

The curious plainsong could be heard
And, grown accustomed to the dark,
Our eyes at last could just remark
Below our window that strange bird.

It fluttered, hovering near the ground,
Pale and large, its body square
With tiny wigs, it trod the air
And danced to its own tuneless sound.

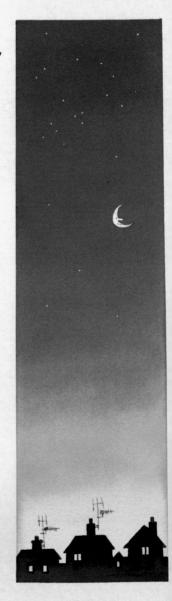

This was a creature of the town
Not found in woods of oak or pine
But on night-hidden washing-line,
The dancing, flapping nightingown.

Vernon Scannell

A Girl on My Swing

I saw a girl on my swing
at the top of the garden.
She had yellow hair
with a red ribbon
and all she did was
swing
swing
swing

so I went to her
and asked her
to be my friend
and she said
"I'm not allowed
to have any friends.
My mother says
ghosts
should keep themselves
to themselves."

swing
swing
swing

Sue Stewart

Night Watch

The moon trudged up the wood.
I waited by the wall till everything
was touched with blue, from shadows dark as ink
to sheet-white grass, my clothes too, and my hands,
this time, this one night.

When further and higher up I suddenly heard
steps – stone against stone, a slither. And again,
stone ground on stone again. Heavy. And again –
Hooves? Feet? Paws? Monster's? Or murderer's?

Which way were they going? Coming?
I strained to tell, a bramble – coil hiding me.
No other sound. Which way? This way yet?
Too scared to move at all I turned into a tree,
a dead tree playing statues with the moon.

Whose steps were up there jostling the stones?
They never came or left. Under a little cliff by day
I found them out. Those feet were never legged –
I found water, playing at life in the drips
of a falling streamlet, marking time.

That night, the moon full –
held still by that cold trick, what did I miss?

Libby Houston

The Old House

The old house stands at the foot of the hill –
Blackened, silent, still.

They say on dark nights
You can hear
The ghost of a laugh,
A cry of fear.

That you can see
Beside the wall
A shadowy figure
Gaunt and tall,
Clutching a bundle
Wrapped in a cloak.

That you can see
The swirling smoke
And hear the crackling
Of the fire
And watch as the flames
Leap higher and higher...

The old house stands at the foot of the hill –
Blackened, silent, still.

John Foster

Haunted Housework

That ghost was such a nuisance
spoiling everyone's demeanour,

until one day and quite by chance,
I whoooooooshed it up in the vacuum cleaner!

Michael Johnson

Is There a Ghost in This Classroom?

Before anything, don't turn around,
ghosts are never where you expect them to be.
Let's look for signs. Does your desk lid
slam unexpectedly while you're carefully closing it?
Do pens and pencils wriggle and squirm
and slip from your fingers and dive to the floor?
And when you look for them, they've disappeared
and no one can find them for weeks and weeks
until they turn up under a radiator
looking much the same but not feeling quite right?
Do the legs of your chair wobble nervously?
Do stacks of exercise books mysteriously slither apart
or your biro suddenly start to write in invisible ink?
And when you're working, do you sometimes sense
someone watching you – and it's not the teacher,
who's looking out of the window, or your friends,
who are watching their hands write – but
somewhere you can't see, but can feel like heat or light,
you know something's eyes are staring into you?
Now tell me, do you feel
a sudden small wind licking your ankles,
a slow cold shiver sliding up your leg?
Is there an icy itch prickling your neck?
Do you hear a soft whispering, so close and quiet
it sounds like it's inside your head? You do?
Then there is a ghost in this classroom
and it's here
to haunt you.

Dave Calder

Witches

Me and Roberta are witches.
She has a really scary witch-dress
made out of a plastic garbage bag
with a place for your head and arms cut out.
I've got a broomstick that is also
a magic wand if I get mad at somebody.
It's still a week until Hallowe'en
but we figure that it's better
to practise being witches for a while
until we get the hang of it.
It's not easy saying witchy things
when you've got a creepy mask
over your mouth with a wart
on the green forehead.
You have to talk crackily and screechily
when putting spells on things.
My brother has a rubber frog and snake
he said I could tie into a necklace
only he won't let me borrow them
until Hallowe'en comes.
Roberta still has to get a witch's hat,
but that's all we need now
unless we find something very frightening
like a realistic fake bat or lizard
before next week.

Julie O'Callaghan

93

Is It a Monster?

Listen to the beasty
Scratching, scratching.
It's going to bite your feeties
Biting, biting.

While you're gently sleeping
It crawls into your bed
Slides between the soft warm sheets
And SMACKS YOU ON THE HEAD.

You lie quite still
It settles down
You try to scream
It turns around.

Feel its hairy body
Moving, moving.
It crawls along your tummy
Crawling, crawling.

You try to move your body
The beasty gives a grin
You scream and scream and scream and scream
Your mum comes running in.

The light's turned on
The beasty growls
You scream again
Your mother howls.

"HOW MANY TIMES HAVE I TOLD YOU
NOT TO LET THE CAT IN YOUR ROOM!"

Anthony Smith

94

It's Behind You

I don't want to scare you
But just behind you
is a...

No! Don't look!
Just act calmly
As if it wasn't there.

Like I said
Can you hear me if I whisper?
Just behind you
Is a...

NO! DON'T LOOK!
Just keep on reading
Don't turn round, believe me
It isn't worth it.

If you could see
What I can see standing there
You'd understand.

It's probably one
Of the harmless sort
Although with that mouth
Not to mention the teeth
And all that blood
Dripping down its chin
I wouldn't like to say.

Oh listen
It's trying to speak
I think it wants to be friends.

Oh I see it doesn't, never mind
You'd better leave just in case
I expect you'll escape
if you don't look round.

Oh what a shame!
I thought you'd make it
To the door. Hard luck.
I still think it means no harm
I expect it bites all its friends.

David Harmer

95

Index of first lines